ONE KIND WORD

WOMEN SHARE THEIR ABORTION STORIES

ONE KIND WORD

WOMEN SHARE THEIR ABORTION STORIES

EDITED BY
Martha Solomon

PHOTOGRAPHS BY
Kathryn Palmateer

THREE O'CLOCK PRESS

Toronto

One Kind Word: Women Share Their Abortion Stories
Edited By Martha Solomon Photographs By Kathryn Palmateer

Library and Archives Canada Cataloguing in Publication

One kind word : women share their abortion stories / edited by Kathryn Palmateer & Martha Solomon ; foreword by Judy Rebick & Jillian Bardsley.

ISBN 978-1-927513-27-9 (pbk.)

1. Abortion—Canada—Psychological aspects. 2. Abortion—Canada. 3. Abortion services—Canada. 4. Reproductive rights—Canada. 5. Women—Canada—Biography. I. Palmateer, Kathryn, editor II. Solomon, Martha, 1973-, editor

HQ767.5.C2O54 2014   362.1988'800971   C2014-901375-2

Printed and bound in Canada by Marquis

For my mother, with gratitude for teaching me what it means to be pro-choice.

—Martha

Beatrice and Thelma. This is for you, my girls. May you always have the right to choose.
And do know, there may come a time when you have to fight hard for that right.
But I will always be there, fighting alongside you.

—Kathryn

FOREWORD

JUDY REBICK

In January 2014 I was listening to a lovely documentary on the radio about theatre students who had written and performed a play about the life of my good friend and pioneer feminist Doris Anderson. Among the many women's issues that Doris fought for was women's reproductive freedom, including the right to abortion. Under her editorial leadership, *Chatelaine* magazine featured articles on abortion in the 1960s when almost no one was talking about it. In 1971, she published an article based on women's stories of abortion and what they suffered because it was illegal and inaccessible. The pro-choice issue was central to Doris's life. So, I was shocked when I heard that the group had decided not to include Doris's pro-choice activism because a few people amongst them were anti-choice. To me, it would be like a theatre group excluding evolution from a history of science because some of their group were creationists.

We won legal abortion in this country in 1988, probably before these young people were born. It was a long and sometimes bitter battle. We fought against governments, police, courts, and most of all the anti-choice. We stood up, spoke out, organized, fundraised, demonstrated, lobbied, and argued against the anti-choice notion that abortion was immoral and shameful. Women seeking abortion went to the Morgentaler clinics across the country, even when they were illegal, even when they had to put up with rude and aggressive anti-choice picketers. Those brave women showed that once you've decided to terminate a pregnancy nothing will stop you. We argued that it was a woman's choice, a private decision in which the state had no role. Most Canadians agreed with us then, and even more agree with us now. Yet, in 2014, a group of pro-feminist students still agreed to exclude abortion from their play.

As part of the movement then, we organized testimonials from women who had desperately sought abortion when it was illegal, or later when it was legalized under such restrictive circumstances that only a small percentage of women who needed abortions got them in safe and supportive conditions. But since the legalization of abortion, there has been too much silence. The anti-choice organizations, who now have a supportive federal government, have continued their vile propaganda, the purpose of which is, at least in part, to make women with an unwanted pregnancy feel guilty if they choose abortion.

That's why I think a book where women go public about their abortions is so important today. One of the reasons I became so active in the pro-choice movement was that it was an area where women's suffering was totally unnecessary. Even in 1988 abortions were safe. Women could have access to all the information they needed to make the decision that was right for them. A woman might have regrets about having an abortion, as we often have regrets about decisions we make, but most women I talked to knew that the decision was the right one for them. Whether they felt grief or not shouldn't be decided by a political debate.

Access to abortion still needs improvement in Canada, but in most provinces, thanks to Dr. Morgentaler and his supporters, it is considered a medical procedure like any other covered by public health insurance. Legal abortion is a unique achievement in Canada. It is the only developed country where there is no abortion law but it seems there is still silence. Breaking that silence is an important step in breaking the veil of shame that continues to surround abortion.

The stories in this volume range from the years that abortion was illegal to quite recently. For some women, the decision was difficult but necessary. Some just knew that they couldn't have a child or another child at that time. Others simply didn't want to have children and still don't. Some had supportive friends and families, some had supportive health care workers, but others faced hostility for their decision. Like any other difficult decision in life, not everyone who loves us or cares for us agrees with our decisions. But with abortion, despite the fact that it is a safe and legal procedure, the judgment is still there. Many of the women writing their stories in this volume believe that judgment comes from the relentless campaigning of the anti-choice.

I also believe that the opposition to women's reproductive freedom is deeply connected to patriarchy, to the notion that women's primary role in society is to reproduce. It's true that many religions ban abortion but those religions are also based on patriarchal beliefs. The Catholic Church, for example, continues its outmoded opposition to artificial means of birth control, as well as abortion under any circumstances. It's not an accident that it also continues to refuse to allow women to be priests. Every fundamentalist religion that I know of places a ban on abortion and restricts the role of women in their ranks.

Because we have won legal abortion in Canada, most women active on the issue have turned to other less successful battles. A new generation of women seems to be placing their focus on violence against women, especially rape culture and women's economic equality. Pro-choice activists continue to keep their eye on the attempts to recriminalize abortion that come from backbench Conservatives from time to time.

So I am glad to see women who are not necessarily engaged in the pro-choice movement speaking out about their experience of abortion. I hope it will encourage other women to be able to speak about their experience to their friends and family.

Judy Rebick is a well-known feminist, social justice activist, author, journalist, and speaker. She is perhaps best known to Canadians as a former president of the National Action Committee on the Status of Women, Canada's largest women's group. Judy was also centrally involved in the battle to legalize abortion in Canada during the 1980s.

FOREWORD

JILLIAN BARDSLEY

Over the past century, health care professionals, activists, women, and allies have worked together to ensure that women and girls are better able to live the lives to which they aspire. Much of this activism has focused on reproductive health care and access to safe abortion. It has been more than twenty-five years since the Morgentaler Decision, a landmark Canadian Supreme Court case that gave women the right to an abortion when they felt they needed one. In North America, approximately one in four clinically recognized pregnancies ends in a therapeutic abortion and approximately one in three women will have an abortion by the time they reach menopause. Aren't these facts evidence enough that a woman's right to choose has become a non-issue? Have we not won the war?

The truth that lies just below the aforementioned statistics is that the movement for accessible abortion is still waiting for a second act. In Canada, abortion is only truly accessible to documented women living in cities who know how to navigate the healthcare system. Young women, undocumented women, and women who live outside of major urban centres continue to struggle to access the services they need. There are women in Canada who are still inducing their own terminations, resulting in significant morbidity and unimaginable pain. There are mothers in the North and rural Canada who must leave their families, jobs, and other responsibilities for days at a time to seek out a procedure that takes approximately fifteen minutes. Outside of Canada, in the developing and developed worlds, women are still dying in attempts to control their futures and make decisions about the welfare of their families. The war has not been won for them.

I have been fortunate enough to grow up in a country and with a family that believes in a woman's right to choose. As a student activist and future physician, I spend a great deal of my time promoting the concept of reproductive justice. What I find fascinating is that despite the legal status of abortion in my community and despite being very publically supportive of abortion rights, outside of my interactions with patients, only one woman from my personal life has ever told me that she has had an abortion. While abortion is theoretically accessible in Canada, the stigma of the procedure looms heavy. This stigma breeds isolation, silence, fear, and uncertainty. However, as several women featured in this book point out, an abortion does not necessarily need to lead to these emotions. While some women may grieve and feel guilt after an abortion, studies have shown that the primary emotion that the majority of women feel after an abortion is relief. It is highly unfortunate that they are not able to speak about their experiences for fear of discrimination and condemnation. The war has also yet to be won for these women. As a society, we need to let women know that we are celebrating their autonomy and the care and responsibility they feel for their futures and families along with them.

I am incredibly grateful and excited for the publication of *One Kind Word*. The women who tell their stories in these pages are trailblazers. They show us that women who have abortions are our mothers, our sisters, our children, our partners, our friends, and ourselves. They are women; simply, they are people. We must continue to strengthen their rights and stop governments and various agencies from imposing new restrictions on access to reproductive health care services. Taking away women's rights in one community does not elevate the status of women in any community.

As a future physician, I place particular value on science and facts. It concerns me that first trimester surgical abortion techniques are discussed in only half of Canada's medical schools. This is a serious issue, as the main barrier to choice in Canada is the absence of trained providers and fifty percent of Canadian abortion providers are over the age of fifty. We must make an effort to train new providers and expand the practice of nurse practitioners and midwives. Unfortunately, there are many bogus "health information sites" and so-called "pregnancy crisis centres" that intentionally misinform women as to the complications of abortion. If medical trainees aren't taught that abortion does not cause breast cancer, infertility, or depression and that the procedure is quick and relatively painless, women will be forced to make decisions without being fully and truthfully informed. As the pro-choice community moves forward, I would like to share some things that I have learned in my studies with you. We know that women who do not wish to be pregnant will attempt to induce an abortion regardless of the legal status or relative safety of the available procedures. We know that women have, on average, four major reasons to terminate their pregnancy and their male partners have three reasons to desire an abortion. As we move forward as a conscientious and intelligent country, I hope we can remember these things and continue to build health policy that respects the autonomy and needs of women. *One Kind Word* does an excellent job of contextualizing the fact that real women will lose if we don't stand our ground and continue to fight for reproductive justice and equality.

We have reasons to be optimistic. Activists, students, and women will continue to push for positive changes. Hopefully, within the next decade, we will be celebrating the ready availability of abortion in Prince Edward Island, New Brunswick, the North, and in rural communities, as well as the licensing of registered nurse practitioners and midwives to perform abortions. However, the second half of the fight for reproductive justice will not be won by increased access and decreased stigma alone. We must work towards truly offering motherhood by choice. For many women, financial concerns and the need for childcare are major factors in whether or not they are ready to raise a or another child. The fight for accessible childcare, equal pay for equal work, and the end of systemic sexism, classism, and cultural violence are all essential battles to be won before we can truly say we are offering women a choice.

Jillian Bardsley holds a Bachelor's of Arts and Science in Women's Studies and Biomedical Science from McGill University. She previously served as the Co-President on the Toronto Chapter of Medical Students for Choice and has been involved in the feminist and pro-choice movements in Toronto and Montreal. Jillian is currently studying medicine at the University of Toronto. She hopes to practice as a family physician and to continue her work with the Canadian pro-choice community.

INTRODUCTION

MARTHA SOLOMON & KATHRYN PALMATEER

"The support I would have appreciated: one kind word from anyone. When I counsel women at the clinic now, I use words like brave, wise, smart, and courageous. I do what I can to communicate to these women that making a choice like this is another step towards empowerment—that they are choosing for themselves." —Lori

Lori's story of her abortion experience is over forty years old and yet seems as though it could have happened yesterday. It was 1972, she was a pregnant teen who needed care and compassion, and instead, she was silenced, judged, and isolated. These feelings remained with her, and today they affect the way she counsels women. To one degree or another, the women who have shared their stories in this book have all felt this same stigma—before, during, and after their abortions. All of them believe that ending the silence surrounding women's abortion experiences is the way to work towards a more open, honest, and compassionate dialogue about abortion in Canada.

In this book you will meet thirty-two Canadian women who have had abortions. They are courageous and brave; they are inspiring; they are our mothers, sisters, friends, lovers, neighbours, teachers, politicians, doctors, and grandmothers. Their experiences reflect the state of reproductive freedom in Canada today. Cumulatively, these women have faced a myriad of issues related to abortion care. They have faced lack of abortion services in their area and access issues due to funding and excessive wait times; they have faced down virulent anti-choicers at clinics and sometimes within their own families and relationships; they have dealt with feelings of isolation, fear, and stigma. All of these women have shared their stories because they are pro-choice and concerned about the state of reproductive freedom in Canada.

Our idea of sharing women's portraits and abortion experiences started in October 2007. After reading an article in the *Ottawa Citizen* about lengthy wait times for abortion services in the Ottawa region, Kathryn was outraged. In her anger, she sent an email to friends and contacts to see who was interested in taking action. Martha answered and the arts4choice project was born. Over the next seven years, we collected women's stories and portraits from all across Canada. As it grew, the project morphed several times—from a website and online gallery, to an exhibit that travelled the country. In 2008, arts4choice received an Ontario Arts Council Multi-Arts Project grant, which allowed us to continue our work and present "Choice Out Loud," a multi-arts event that included, film, dance, portraits, and stories. Arts4choice was also featured in the *Globe and Mail* story "Choosing Silence" by Cate Cochran in July 2008 and was part of an article in *Chatelaine* magazine in 2009.

When we began, we knew we wanted to break down the feelings of isolation and fear that many women experience because of the stigma attached to abortion. We also wanted to address and refute the idea that an abortion is a shameful experience and combat the misogynist messages perpetuated by the anti-choice movement, which depicts women who have had abortions as either heartless monsters or hapless victims. We were also eager to address the lack of women's voices in discussions of abortion—in the media and in policy debates. Most of all, though, we wanted women to feel comfortable talking to each other about their abortion experiences. We felt that these goals were best served by giving women a platform to share their experiences, not only with each other but with a larger audience as well.

We felt that combining women's stories, told in their own words, with their photographic portraits was the most powerful means of addressing these issues. We believed that this combination was the most personal and intimate way to refute stereotypes about women who have had abortions. In essence, we wanted to create a space where readers could "meet" the women sharing their stories.

At first, we wondered if women would be willing to share their stories and portraits with a larger audience. Were we asking too much? Would women be willing to go public in this way? To our delight, they were! We have had overwhelmingly positive reactions to our callouts for participants and to the project in general. When women see other women publicly sharing their experiences, it chips away at the stigma and fear that surround the abortion experience and encourages more women to come forward. Courage is contagious.

Amanda recalls first seeing the project and then deciding to become a participant:

> "When I originally saw the *Globe and Mail* article that featured this project, I was so impressed! I thought: those women are SO BRAVE. What a courageous thing to do, what a brilliant project to put a positive light on abortion. To say 'Yes, I have had an abortion and that is okay. Abortion is not a shameful thing.' When I had the chance to be a part of this project, I thought: this is something I need to do. I am so proud of the women who stand up and speak out and get photographed for this cause. This is something that I want to be a part of."

The responses we have had from people all over the country, and around the world, have made it evident that this is a project whose time has come. Women are refusing to be silenced and shamed because they have exercised their right to reproductive freedom. Women who have experienced abortions want to reach out to each other and talk openly about their experiences. If they felt isolated, silenced, or shamed during or after their experience, they passionately want to ensure that other women do not have similar experiences. Sheila writes:

> "The solidarity demonstrated through the existence of this arts project will offer some comfort and empowerment to women who have been silenced for whatever reason because they will hear and see themselves in these stories and photos and know that they are not alone.... I also hope the arts4choice stories and photos will help to shift negative attitudes toward us and improve women's access to safe, timely, and free abortions."

An enormous part of the appeal of this project is that it includes portraits. The women who have shared their experiences have also shared their identities. They have put a face to their experiences. Sharing our experiences is important, but claiming them is powerful too. Doing so is a determined rejection of the shame and secrecy the anti-choice movement would like to impose upon women. Jennifer writes:

"I think it's important to be open about it. I think people are very drawn to photography, as it's a medium that can be extremely personal because you can look people in the eye through the photo. I wanted to be part of this project because I think it's so important for people to see that choosing abortion comes from a place of compassion and that it could be anyone making the choice."

However, it is the powerful combination of portraits and stories, presented in tandem, that destroys any misogynist stereotypes perpetuated by the anti-choice movement. Sheila explains:

"Photos complementing our written stories, particularly a collection of women's photos and stories like arts4choice is producing (rather than an individual story like mine), is even more dramatic in its effect because the visual dimension will help people see and process more comprehensively that we are everywhere, and we are various ages from different racial, class, and cultural backgrounds. Through the photos, they will see people who look like their friends, coworkers, sisters, etcetera. This association of familiarity will help them to feel some empathy, or possibly even a little compassion."

Politically, putting one's face and story "out there" is a radical way to flip the script on abortion. Abortion in Canada today is about women making a health care decision that is right for them and their families. It can be a hard choice, an easy choice, a conflicted choice, or a choice filled with relief. It can even be all these things at once. When women share their real experiences, it serves to complicate an overly simplified narrative about abortion. It shows that reproductive freedoms are important because women's lives are complex, unique, and precious.

In terms of abortion access, Canada is unique. Canada does not have any legislation that governs access to abortion and the majority of abortions performed in Canada are covered by provincial health care plans. In this way, we appear to be a testament to the power of allowing women to decide for themselves if they should have an abortion, without invasions into their privacy, threats of criminal charges, unsafe procedures, or exorbitant fees. However, barriers to access are a very real and disturbing problem in Canada today. For example, women in remote and rural areas still face the burden of needless wait times, extra appointments, and out-of-pocket travel expenses. Privacy is often non-existent in smaller towns and remote areas, and if women encounter anti-choice resistance, they have little to no recourse. Even in larger towns and urban areas, women have difficulty navigating the system and often end up dealing with anti-choice pregnancy crisis centers that shame, threaten, and humiliate women. The inequities of abortion access mirror the greater inequities of our society. Colonialism and racism can severely affect women's abortion access and experiences. Low-income women face greater barriers than do affluent women, and access is even more tenuous for homeless, refugee, and undocumented women.

In many parts of the country, there are simply no providers available; in others, such as Prince Edward Island, provincial health authorities have refused to honour women's basic reproductive health care needs and do not fund abortion services. Women from PEI who require an abortion must travel to another province and fund the costs of their abortion and travel expenses themselves. In New Brunswick, a woman must have the approval of two doctors before obtaining a provincially funded abortion. Sadly, the Fredericton Morgentaler clinic, the only other option for women seeking abortions in the maritimes, is scheduled to close in July 2014 after years of fighting the New Brunswick government, thus further limiting the already paltry options for east coast women. In no other area of health care would such an egregious disrespect for people's basic health care needs be tolerated. Indeed, the problems with access in Canada point to a deep-seated misogyny within our country and our health care system.

These problems—issues of privacy, financial hardships, lengthy wait times, scheduling barriers, and anti-choice harassment—are part of many (if not most) of the stories you will read in this book. While, quite rightly, most of our pro-choice efforts in Canada tend to focus on these issues, our project has highlighted another area that needs attention: quality of care. Women's abortion experiences, much like their access to the services themselves, are often dependent upon their location and their luck. Do you live in a major urban area? Do you live in a remote Northern community? Does your province provide abortion services? Was the nurse at the hospital pro-choice? Does your family doctor provide referrals for abortions? Do you have someone to take you home after your abortion? Did the doctor provide compassionate care? Were there anti-choice protesters harassing clients? All of these can make a huge impact on the quality of care women receive and how women evaluate their experiences.

This project is just the beginning of a move towards addressing how the kind of care women need and expect measures up to the care they actually receive (if they are even able to access it). Access to abortion care is the bare minimum, and we must aim higher to ensure that women's reproductive freedoms are respected in this country. It is time for women themselves to articulate what kind of abortion care this country requires. We need to ask ourselves: what is it about our experiences that we need to keep, and what do we need to change? We can only do that when we are open and vocal about our experiences, both positive and negative. In this way, we can expand our vision of what comprehensive, feminist, on-demand abortion care can and should look like in this country, and we can also work towards building a stronger, more inclusive, and more authentic conversation about reproductive justice in Canada.

In our outreach, we tried to find participants from a diversity of backgrounds in hopes of showing readers that abortion access and experiences can be affected by a great many variables. Our participants come from a range of class backgrounds, ethnicities, abilities, and language groups. You will read stories from Latina women, French Canadians, and First Nations women, as well as women from Asian, Indo-Caribbean, and African Canadian communities. Our participants are young and old (and in-between), financially stable and just making ends meet, mothers and childless, in relationships and single, heterosexual and lesbian. Is this book as diverse as we would like it to be? Not even close. This project is only the beginning of what we hope will be a larger move towards sharing our abortion experiences with each other. Our hope is that projects such as this one will continue to grow, become more diverse, and more representative of all Canadian women.

Sometimes, being a pro-choice activist can be depressing and overwhelming. Anti-choicers routinely lie, harass, assault, and bully, often with impunity. It takes its toll—on women, on activists, on providers, on clinic escorts, on the possibility of any open, rational discussion about reproductive freedoms. Indeed, in the beginning, our project was fuelled by a sense of outrage—at lengthy wait times, about the vitriolic misogyny and outright lies of the anti-choice movement, at the complete absence of abortion services for women in many parts of Canada, at the casual judgments made about women who have had abortions. In many ways, this project has been an antidote to this outrage, to the feelings of anger and hopelessness. Instead of viewing the abortion debate as a depressing foray into misogyny, harassment, and lies, this project has become a life-affirming, community-building experience, full of compassion and strength. It has grown from a place of anger and despair into something inspiring, hopeful, compassionate, and deeply moving.

As you read the stories in this book, you will see that each abortion experience is as unique as the woman who relays it. However, all these stories touch on issues that highlight the state of reproductive freedom in Canada today. Our title is taken from Lori's story, a particularly heartfelt and detailed account of her experience of an unplanned pregnancy as a teenager. It was 1972, before Morgentaler, and while abortion was criminalized in the majority of Canadian provinces, she was "lucky" to live in British Columbia. However, at this time in BC, she required both parental permission and the consent of a Therapeutic Abortion Committee. Throughout the experience, she was silenced, judged, and isolated by both health care providers and her family. However, like many other women, she knew that these experiences were plainly wrong and unjust. Later in life, she would address them by providing more compassionate care to women in similar situations. In essence, that is exactly what each woman in this book is doing: providing more compassion, openness, and kindness than they were given.

From the very early stages of the project, one of our goals was to have a copy of this book in every clinic waiting room across the country. Our hope was that we could get these stories into the hands of women who would find them helpful, inspiring, useful: women who have had abortions, women considering an abortion, women who have decided to have an abortion. We hope that these stories resonate with you and help you to engage in more open dialogues about women's abortion experiences—whether they are your own experiences or those of your friends, family, or community members. Let's move together towards more equitable, caring, and just abortion care in Canada. Courage is contagious.

WHITEFEATHER

I want to break down any stereotypes about the "types" of women who have abortions or work to protect abortion rights. I am well educated, informed, empowered, and have a family that includes a planned child.

My first abortion happened when I was nineteen. I was dating a man who physically abused me. I had planned to carry the pregnancy to full term, but the physical abuse escalated and I decided to terminate the pregnancy. My second abortion happened when I was twenty-five. I already had a two-year-old child. The prospect of raising a second child alone as a single mother already on welfare was an impossible thought. The child I had already was a planned child, but my marriage had dissolved and I was struggling as it was.

I had full access, although, in New Brunswick, women must have the approval of two doctors. If my doctor had not been a compassionate feminist, the process would have been much more intimidating and difficult. I've seen first-hand that this legislation has meant limited access for other women in NB, where religious influence interferes with women's reproductive rights.

Both of my abortions were not easy decisions to make, but I was firm in my decision once I had made it. I love babies, and the notion of the potential for a baby in my life had emotional attachments that I had to deal with. I wrote a lot of poetry about it and performed it publicly as a way of voicing my experiences. At the time, I felt the abortions were necessary and that I was giving both my son and myself a second and third chance at a decent life. I still feel grateful and relieved about my decision, both times I had to make it.

NICOLE

I think that women will always attempt to end pregnancies when in need and there should be safe ways for them to do so.

I was about twenty-one and in a relationship. I was living on my own and in school. I really did not involve anyone except a friend of mine and the guy involved. I immediately told him I was having an abortion and he agreed. I decided the minute I realized that I had missed a few periods. The guy was not who I wanted for the father of my child.

Nothing else crossed my mind and I really felt no connection to the pregnancy. I still feel nothing for it. It was just not for me and I knew it. I did not feel guilty, but I fully understand women that do. It is not something that you typically plan and you are allowed to feel what you need to.

I don't talk about it because I want to avoid judgment. When I hear people talk about it, they make having an abortion sound like such a horrible loss. For me it was a means to an end, and I have found it hard to explain that mindset to people. I'm not interested in defending my personal choice to people that may never understand.

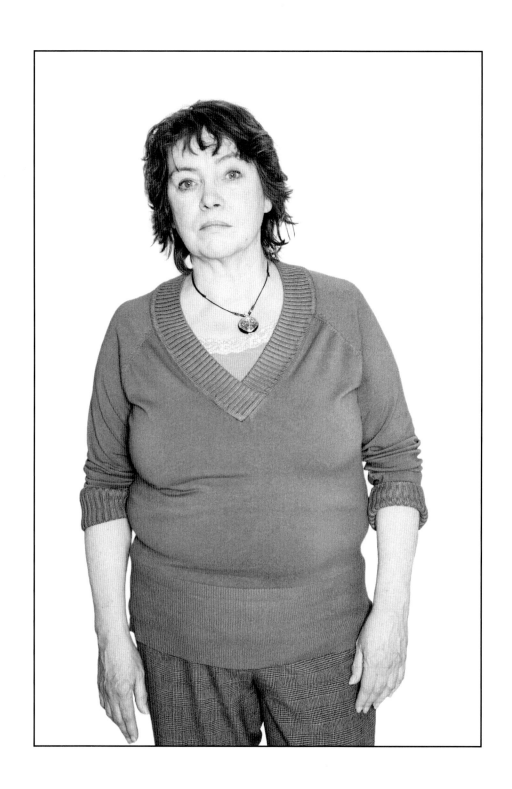

LINDA

I had an abortion in 1968 when I was twenty-two years old. Abortion was not legal and it was a terrifying experience. You had to ask through the grapevine until you finally met someone, who knew someone, who knew someone….

When I didn't heal well after the abortion I was terrified to go to the doctor because it was illegal. What if I got arrested? What if I was forced to report the abortionist's name? No one should have to go through this experience. I finally went to Women's College Hospital where I was treated with kindness.

I think we need to stand up and be counted. We need to be seen—a diverse group of women from all ages, cultures, and walks of life that have had abortions. I am not ashamed to tell my young daughters about my experience.

GISELLE

Tenia veintidós años de edad cuando estudiaba en la Universidad. Vivía con mi pareja; era una relación de más de dos años más o menos. Dormía entre mi casa y la de él.

Supe la noticia de que estaba embarazada en un Hospital especializado en mujeres. Lo compartí con mis padres y mi pareja. Decidí no tenerlo. Fue una decisión dura, pero sabía que no estaba lista para ser madre.

El proceso fue doloroso pero rápido. No estaba sola, pero me sentía así. Dormí el resto del día y descansé. Al otro día me sentí físicamente bien, pero en mi mente pensaba e imaginaba como hubiera sido lo contrario, pero no me arrepiento.

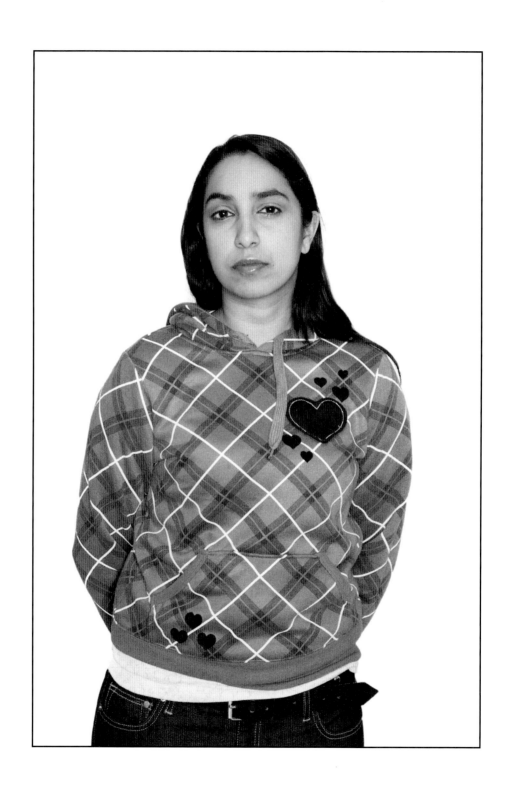

DEB

As a young, indo-caribbean woman, I am a less common face of wimmin who have or access abortions in my community. While there are, in fact, many Brown wimmin who have them, this may not be seen in my own or in white communities.

As a woman who had an abortion at twenty-four years old (I am twenty-nine now), it is important to see that not only teenagers "should" be having abortions. Wimmin of all ages can still choose whether or not they want to take on the role of being a mother.

Abortion is not openly discussed because society wants to control our bodies and what we do with them. So, when and if wimmin are brave enough to speak out about it, they get chastised and disrespected for making a decision that concerns themselves first, not the "unborn child."

I am lucky to be in environments that allow me to talk about my experiences without shame or guilt. Wimmin are told that if they don't feel guilt or shame, then they are cold or callous. Or they are told they must feel like they lost something, as opposed to having gained something else for making that decision.

J.

I want to help take away the shame of abortion. Many women have had one for many reasons. Coming out will help others feel less bad about their decision and remind people that we need to keep working towards safe, accessible abortions in Canada. I want to put a face to it.

I was twenty-seven. The pregnancy was the result of a short relationship while travelling. He lives in another country and I never told him (I found out after I got home). I was starting a new job, a new relationship, and was just not ready to become a parent. I did go on to have three beautiful babies.

I think that we are expected to feel badly about it, even to regret it to a certain extent. I do not feel badly. I hate that I had to make the decision but I feel that I made the right one.

AMBER

We need to fight the notion that abortion is something shameful, something that we must hide and feel guilty about. I have to admit that I felt very little about it. I did not experience guilt or sadness. Mostly, I felt grateful that I had access to the service, but I also felt that it was my right to have it. I continue to be relieved that I was able to have an abortion when I needed one.

I think we are trained to feel guilty, or sad. That being said, I understand that for some women, abortion can be an emotionally difficult experience, and I respect that. At the same time, however, I wonder to what extent these feelings are influenced by the way abortion is treated in the broader society. If we weren't told that we should feel guilty or sad, and that we might need counseling, and that it might be an emotionally trying experience, would we feel this way at all?

It's politically charged, yes, but it's not inherently political. It's a basic healthcare service, and we should be able to talk about it.

SHARON

I am a mother of four great people.
I am also an elected woman in civic government.
I have had an abortion.

MELISA

When I found out I was pregnant at a Coffee Time washroom, I was confused and shocked that it was happening to me, but, in my gut, I knew what I really wanted to do.

I didn't want a child—not with the person I got pregnant with and, generally, I was not prepared to take care of a child.

I made the decision. No one else did. ME. This was a radical experience—knowing that only I could REALLY make that decision because it was my pregnancy. Radical.

I was emboldened by my decision. I became even more angry when I thought of the millions of women that cannot make this decision freely and safely, like I did.

That's why I am willing to speak openly about abortion—I want other women to know that I had one. When I was going through it and decided to tell people, more and more women started telling me they had one. So many women go through this alone, sometimes feeling guilty or thinking that they are the only ones. The abortion clinic was full of women like me, and we looked at each other wondering what we were thinking and feeling.

JEANETTE

It was 1991 and I was twenty years old and not in a relationship.

My pregnancy was a result of sexual assault, and for the first years following the experience, I would always preface my abortion disclosure with that bit of information. "I was raped. I had an abortion." Then it hit me one day that I was being a total hypocrite. I finally owned up to the fact that even if I hadn't been raped, I would have had an abortion. Period.

I realize now that I was letting the anti-choice perspective frame the language around my experience. When I talk about my abortion today, I don't talk about the events that lead up to it.

In order to have an abortion at no cost at the Victoria General Hospital in Halifax, I would have needed a referral from my GP. Since my sister worked at the GP's clinic and I didn't feel comfortable with her knowing I was planning to have an abortion (as the administrative person, she had access to my file and would routinely read it), I had to go to a private clinic. This meant I had to pay the $400 fee, since abortions were not publicly funded out-of-hospital in Nova Scotia at the time. I had to go begging for the money (through the friend who had introduced us) to the person who had raped me. He was happy to absolve himself and paid. But what if he hadn't? Where in the world would I have come up with that money?

There was never a doubt in my mind about terminating the pregnancy. The instant I found out I was pregnant, I went into survival mode. Nothing and nobody was going to stop me from having an abortion. I've never regretted my decision. I'm grateful for that period in my life. It made me who I am today, and I like who I am.

CINDY

There is still so much stigma and shame around abortion. There's a persistent idea that abortion should only be used as a last resort. It's like if you are past a certain age, in a "stable" relationship, have a steady job, or already have kids, you're not as entitled to an abortion as folks who are not. Whatever happened to "on demand"?

Women face incredible challenges around abortion: stigma, shame, and misinformation propagated by the anti-abortion movement, such as "links" between abortion and breast cancer and reduced fertility. Women also face pressure, lack of support from partners and/or family, dubious access to services, feeling like "they should've known better," self-blame, and having to justify their decision and the reasons behind it.

Thankfully, I had always been pro-choice, was active in an adamantly pro-choice feminist organization, and knew how to navigate abortion services, so it was easier for me to initiate the abortion process. I also lived in a major city where abortion services are relatively easily accessed and had a valid health card.

I was very, very clear that I did not want a baby at the time, wasn't ready for one, and certainly didn't want to be in a long-term relationship with the person I was with.

At this stage in my life, I'm trying to get pregnant with a female partner and it's been a trying and difficult process, so I continue to be adamant about reproductive rights and control, although from an entirely different angle. But no matter how hard I struggle to get pregnant now, I have never once regretted having an abortion.

It always feels good to talk about it, getting together with women and refusing to feel shame. I wish it would happen more.

ELIZABETH

I was living in a different city than my mom. I was in my first year at a new high school and I connected with a girl at school who had also been through it. She took me to the doctor. But in order to get an abortion I had to tell my parents because I was only fifteen.

The doctor removed me from my mom and took me into a private room and questioned me. She asked me if I was okay killing another living being. It was disturbing.

I said, "I would rather keep my life going in a forward direction than bring something into the world that I am not prepared to take care of."

There's a lot of guilt attached to having an abortion, and somehow it's not about women's bodies. Society tends to remove all care from the body of the woman and place it on the fetus.

JAIME

I've never felt politically or personally silenced until this abortion happened, and now I see that oppression and suppression are alive and well in the world.

I had a lot of support from the women at the clinic. They had the doctor come in and speak with me, as I told them I had a phobia of doctors and wasn't sure I could go through with it. The doctor was calm and gentle and she made me feel more comfortable than I have ever felt with a doctor. The counselor that spoke with me before the procedure stayed with me the whole time I was there, during the procedure, and if it wasn't for her support I don't think I could have done it, even though I knew it was the right thing for me to do at the time. I also had a lot of support from my boyfriend, who helped me have the courage to do what was right for me. I really appreciated the support of all these people. What would I have done without them?

I am furious that I am not able to grieve without feeling like I will be misinterpreted politically. I am very angry that politics dictate how I should be feeling about my decision. I just want to be able to feel what I feel, without being told to cheer up, or not worry, that I did the right thing or the wrong thing. I just want the space and the support to go through this naturally and not feel pressured in any way.

I make myself discuss this openly because I think it is very important for women to feel a sense of community and draw strength from each other.

PAIGE

I was eighteen and in my last year of high school. I was living with my parents and I was in an abusive relationship. This person wanted me to have a baby and it was terrifying to tell him that that was not going to happen.

My boyfriend at that time was very hostile and very anti-choice. I had to deal with him calling me a "baby-killer" and other unkind comments.

I had a lot of support from my mom, who is very pro-choice. I had some support from friends, but like many women, I didn't tell many people because of the shame. As well, my friends and I were young, so I didn't know who to ask for support and my friends didn't know how to give it. As an adult, when friends of mine are faced with an unplanned pregnancy, I have been sure to ask them what kind of support I can provide them.

There is still so much stigma around abortion. How can we talk about abortion when we don't even have permission to really talk about, have, pursue, or enjoy sex? Our sexual freedom has improved, but when you look at the current US government and the Christian right, you realize that in many ways we are still in the dark ages.

How does this make me feel?
Really fucking angry.

MÉLANIE

At the time I felt angry and upset. I felt like I didn't have a choice at all...despite all the options (abortion, have a baby and keep it, give it up for adoption). I just felt resentful about being in the position of having to make this decision. And then on the flip side I felt shame and guilt and punished myself, telling myself that I got myself into this situation and had no right to be upset or resentful.

I was very repressed emotionally at the time, so I buried a lot of my feelings. Still, it caught me off guard that it messed with my head more than I thought it would. That being said—while I was surprised by suddenly weighing all the options—I knew, in the end, that I didn't want a baby. I still don't want babies. I think I made the right decision and don't regret it. I wish I could have dealt with it better mentally and emotionally at the time, but it's a journey and a process.... I did the best I could then.

I have a tattoo on my belly. It is Hebrew and says, "I shall be with you in the spirit" (the man I got pregnant with was Jewish). It is a tribute to the spirit baby. Many strangers or acquaintances will ask what it means and why I have it.

JENNIFER

I had just turned twenty-eight and was with my boyfriend (who is my husband now). We had been together for four years at the time and we just weren't ready at that point in our lives. We talked about it a lot, and having an abortion was the right choice for me and for us, it was pretty clear. We were both working, but I had made the decision to go back to school. It wasn't the right time, I was extremely sick, and it just didn't feel right. I am grateful for the choice that I made.

I had my abortion at a clinic. I had the most amazing support from my boyfriend and a few dear friends before and after the abortion. It was extremely helpful to have their support and know that I could talk openly about what I was going through. I had a brief counseling session before my procedure that I found extremely helpful, and from there I found it relatively easy to move forward with my life.

Although abortion is legal in Canada, services vary province to province, making it extremely complicated to navigate the system in an efficient and dignified manner. Often, women are forced to carry the weight of this decision with little support, and depending on what government is in power, choice seems to be ever threatened. We need to create a society where women's choices are supported and celebrated, not undermined and judged.

LAURA

It's funny that I still get that tummy queasiness, considering it's not a secret with my family or my friends that I've had an abortion....

I don't know why I still hesitate to be public about it, since I sure don't hesitate to say what I think about abortion access. So I'm willing to get my picture taken because I think I have to get over this fear of being publicly "outed."

I walked through a throng of anti-choice protesters on my way into the clinic and I've shouted them down in rallies. Why should this be harder? I don't think I'm silent but obviously we're not out there enough if people think we're silent, stigmatized, and have no one to stand up for us. What about standing up for ourselves?

To say that Canadians just don't think about abortion anymore...duh! If you need one and can't get one, you think about it. If you need one and got one, you think about it. If you know someone who got one, you think about it. If your period is three days late and you wonder what the hell you'll do "if," you think about it.

KITTY

I was eighteen years old, in an unstable relationship, living with my mother, and working part-time while going to college full-time.

The doctor that was meant to perform the abortion cancelled my appointment at the last minute and was unable to offer another appointment until after I was over thirteen weeks along (his cut-off). I kicked up so much of a fuss that his secretary ended up scheduling my appointment at the clinic.

It was and still is the absolutely right decision for me.

Some people seemed perturbed by the fact that I was not more "cut up" by the whole experience, which frustrated me.

I found that my talking gave others "permission" to be open about what they were experiencing.

SHEILA

I was twenty-three years old, in a relationship, living on my own, and just finishing my BSc. It was 1986 and there was still the "tribunal system" that required my doctor to send the request for a therapeutic abortion to a three-doctor review panel. This freaked me out, the possibility of denial.

When we got the result and I asked right away how to get an abortion, my male doctor asked me if I didn't love my boyfriend. I was furious and got through the appointment with civility only to get him to send the request to the tribunal. I never saw that doctor again (my choice). I knew it was right as soon as he said that the test was positive, and in twenty-two years, I've never looked back. I am really glad I could make that choice.

I think it's so very important for women who are willing and able to share the stories of their abortions—and all aspects of their/our lives—because our personal stories are political stories. It can take a lot of courage to expose yourself, to place yourself in that vulnerable position, and yet, in the right circumstances, where there is political and emotional support, it can also be very empowering and liberating.

DARLENE

We must publicly claim our reproductive rights and stop being afraid or ashamed.

As a graduate student and single parent with two children, I faced an unwanted pregnancy, as my birth control failed.

I was 38 years old and in the middle of my PhD with no money and an already huge student loan debt. I was not in a position to have another child. In light of this, I opted for an abortion.

My partner (then and now) and I went to the Morgentaler Clinic in Toronto, and Dr. Morgentaler himself performed the abortion. In the clinic, I was treated with warmth and human kindness.

This abortion allowed me to put in place a future for myself and the two children I already had.

ANNIE

Mon avortement a eu lieu le 6 novembre 1998. J'avais dix-huit ans, en treizième année, avec une vision qui s'échelonnait sur les cinq prochaines années (côté carrière et études). Je ne prenais aucune contraception hormonale, et j'avais des relations sexuelles non protégées avec mon copain de trois mois. Avec un peu de recul, je suis contente d'avoir discuté d'une grossesse non planifiée avec mon copain avant que ça arrive. Nous étions tous les deux d'accord que notre choix serait l'avortement si cette situation devait survenir. Mes menstruations n'étaient pas toujours à date, pourtant, j'avais un près sentiment d'être en retard. J'ai fait l'achat d'un kit maison, qui a confirmé que j'étais bel et bien enceinte. J'ai pris un test sanguine à la clinique pour confirmer le tout (ma tante qui travaillait là a pris mon test sanguine, mais je savais qu'elle devait garder le tout confidentiel). Lorsque le test est revenu positif pour une grossesse, le docteur m'a référée à un gynécologue.

A l'époque, je n'étais pas au courant que les jeunes filles qui allaient de l'avant avec un avortement étaient victimes de discrimination. La réceptioniste qui a pris mon rendez-vous pour l'avortement m'a demandé si j'allais aussi me faire liguer les trompes. Ce n'est que plusieurs années plus tard que j'ai vraiement compris ce qu'elle voulait dire.

Je ne l'ai pas dit à mes parents pendant 6 ans, portant, les mères sont un don de toujours savoir ce qui ce passe et quand je l'ai admis, elle m'a dit qu'elle l'avait toujours su, mais qu'elle respectait ma décision de ne pas dévoiler que j'avais eu un avortement pendant toutes ces années. Mon copain à l'époque était vraiment bien—il est venu à l'hôpital avec moi, ainsi qu'à tous les rendez-vous—mais après l'avortement, il ne voulait plus en parler, ce qui était vraiment difficile pour moi. Venant d'un petit village (et d'une école Catholique), je n'avais pas de groupe de soutien. La première fois que j'ai vraiment eu la chance d'en parler à quelqu'un était un an passé, quand j'ai commencé a faire du bénévolat à Planning des Naissances d'Ottawa. Ça m'a fait beaucoup de bien d'en parler.

TABATHA

My abortion was over a decade ago and, for the better part of the last ten years, it has been something that I seldom think about. Recently, I have started thinking about my choice more and more, and suddenly I want to talk about it but there isn't anyone around who knows. Maybe I feel safer talking to strangers and sharing my experiences with people I have never met—and this project is one way of sharing my story with people I have never met. I also believe that I need to put my mouth where my heart is. This is something that I am willing to stand up and say is important. It is something that is important about me.

I was really disappointed with my experience at the clinic. After I had "recovered" and was being ushered out, I was pulled over by a nurse and, in front of all the other women who were also "recovering," was told what I should or should not do or expect. She also proceeded to tell me that if I was going to engage in "reckless behavior" I should be on the pill. She didn't think that my reason for being pregnant was "good enough."

It is my body. Why should I be empowered to make decisions about every other aspect of my body and life but this? I actually think that pro-choice is pro-life—the life of the woman! I chose my life.

AMANDA

I was twenty-three years old. Married. Living with my (now ex) husband and our three-year-old son. We were both working at the time, but money was very tight. When I found out I was pregnant, I gave the situation a lot of thought and realized that I was not ready to become a parent of a second child. A big part of the decision was that our marriage was so unstable by that time.

I always considered it a private, medical procedure. But now, after getting involved with this project, I realize that by not talking about it I am encouraging the silence that is associated with the shame and stigma many people try to assign to abortion.

When I originally saw the *Globe and Mail* article that featured this project, I was so impressed! I thought, *Those women are SO BRAVE.* What a courageous thing to do! To say: "Yes, I have had an abortion and that is okay. Abortion is not a shameful thing." When I had the chance to be a part of this project, I thought, *This is something I need to do.* I am so proud of the women who stand up and speak out and get photographed for this cause. This is something that I want to be a part of.

It's been a positive thing for me to hear other women talk frankly and openly about their abortions. It made me realize that it is okay to talk about it, and that I too can help break down that stigma by talking about abortion. It made me want to get involved in this photo project because I can give pro-choice women a "face" by having my photo taken, and hopefully help other women realize that abortion is an okay choice to make if it feels right for them.

ERIN

I found out I was pregnant just as I was starting my second year of medical school. I remember thinking that I should have known better, since I was less than two years away from being a doctor.

For me, the choice was already made—I wasn't ready to have a baby logistically, emotionally, or financially.

I think women are pressured to feel like they should just get over it and move on. They didn't want the baby, so why should they grieve or feel sad? They should feel only relief. That makes me sad. There are so many emotions that go into ending a pregnancy; women should feel however they want. They shouldn't feel guilt over not feeling guilt, either.

I don't feel regret or guilt, just sadness that it had to happen. Despite what anyone might think, I can't wait to have children when the time is right for me. I'm sad that my first pregnancy had to be a secret—you assume it will be this wonderful, celebrated experience. In that way, having an abortion changed my life story, but it hasn't, and won't, change who I am.

I wish more women could talk about their experiences, because I think we all need support from others who can say, "Yeah, me too." If I can use my experience to help others, it will be worth it.

I am proud to call myself a pro-choice doctor-to-be.

SHAWNA

I found a number for my aunt's family doctor and called to make an appointment regarding my irregular periods. When I got to the office I explained what was really going on and they gave me a test and a pelvic exam. They said that they would call if the test was positive.

When I didn't hear from them for the next two weeks I figured everything was fine but was starting to feel symptoms of pregnancy. When I called the office to see if the test had come back positive, they said, "Oh yes, we must have forgotten to call you." When I asked them how I go about getting an abortion they said to look in the Yellow Pages. I finally found a number for a local doctor performing abortions out of the hospital in Sudbury. He advised me I was eleven weeks and that I was only able to make an appointment for the next week.

If the original doctor had been more supportive there wouldn't have been such a rush in the end making it very stressful.

I didn't tell anyone until the day of the abortion, but I had been told that I needed someone to pick me up, so I told my grandmother and aunt who were very supportive. Even though they are both Catholic, they did whatever I needed and did not impose what they thought I should or shouldn't do.

JOYCE

It was January 1988. I was eight weeks pregnant before I realized it, as I had what seemed to be a light period at the normal time the month before. I felt devastated, but knew pretty much right away I wanted an abortion, since I simply wasn't interested in being a mother (and never have been). I made an appointment with my gynecologist, who, by the luck of the draw, was a kindly old fellow near retirement and unquestionably pro-choice. He made all the arrangements with the Therapeutic Abortion Committee at Vancouver General Hospital and assured me that my abortion request would be rubber-stamped. This greatly relieved me, as I was afraid to be turned down and I had no control over the process.

The abortion was scheduled for me, but I had to wait three weeks, because others further along were ahead of me. I know now that three weeks is not nearly as long as many women had to wait, but it felt like an eternity to me. I was sick and miserable with morning sickness the whole time and felt physically awful. I desperately did not want to be pregnant anymore, and could hardly wait to have my abortion. I agonized over things like, *What if the doctor is sick that day? What if the hospital cancels my abortion?*

I had my abortion a few days later in early February, under general anesthetic. I remember waking up afterwards, groggy, but instantly noticed that I felt better physically. The nausea was completely gone. It was such a huge relief—the relief just flooded over me as I was lying there still groggy. After recovering for a couple of hours, they released me. I felt a million times better emotionally, like a huge weight had been lifted off my shoulders. Although it was early February, I remember it was a beautiful, spring-like day, and I went for a walk in the warm sunshine. I felt sublimely happy and appreciative of everything around me, and of having my life back.

I felt strongly that the abortion was the right decision, and I never wavered from that decision from the start. I was very satisfied with my decision—it was the only one for me—and I still am satisfied. I've never had any regrets.

I think women expect to feel a certain way about their abortions. For example, clinic counselors often say that women are surprised that they don't feel guilty and wonder if there's something wrong with them. Women also expect to be treated shabbily or with contempt, and are surprised to get professional, compassionate care at a clinic. This all comes from anti-choice, patriarchal beliefs about motherhood and abortion, which are so wrong and unjust. I suppose I was somewhat infected by the shame and stigma a bit too, at least at the time, since I was reluctant to tell anybody. I feel quite differently now, because of my political evolution and experience, and my ethical understanding of the significance of abortion rights to women.

For years, no one knew about my abortion. Over time, I told a few friends now and then. A few years after I became a pro-choice activist and media spokesperson, I started talking in public about it. Overall, I think my abortion had a very positive effect on my life. I can't say it's the reason I became a pro-choice activist—there were other factors—but it's definitely part of it.

TANYA

I was twenty-two years old. I was living in Vancouver away from family and friends. I got pregnant from a friend of mine, during a brief affair. He was married and I was not ready for a child.

I had the abortion at the Morgentaler Clinic in Winnipeg. I had known about the Morgentaler Clinic because, growing up in Winnipeg, it was a very controversial clinic. It was in the papers a lot for people protesting its existence, and Dr. Morgentaler was a well-known figure in town. I knew where the clinic was and found it very accessible, although it was expensive for a "starving" university student ($500).

I had no anti-choice interference from protestors, family, or friends.

When I was faced with the decision to have an abortion, I knew it was the right thing to do; I was not ready to be a mother. Now, I still feel the same. I have two children, and I don't regret my abortion.

I am pro-choice because I was given the choice, and it has changed my life for the better. I can't imagine not having autonomy over my body, my person.

I am very frustrated with the lack of openness and feel sad that more women can't share their experiences. I found out through my grandmother that my mother had an abortion when she was sixteen years old and during my abortion experience she never told me. I would have loved to hear my mother's experience, because it would have alleviated my shame and isolation.

SUSAN

I had an abortion in 1974.

I was twenty-six and I was married, living with my husband.

I had a baby who was five months old and custody of my husband's angry nine-year-old son.

It was at Toronto East General Hospital. I arranged it by calling a distress centre hotline and OHIP paid for it. There was a preliminary doctor's visit, a hospital stay, and then a follow-up appointment. I felt guilt and relief and enormous sorrow. It was the right thing to do.

I am intelligent and I can make my own decisions about my life and my body.

JILLIAN

I believe that a woman has choice over her body and life. And that choice is only the woman's. The stories of women I've heard make me feel less alone. I am inspired by their bravery and honesty in the face of threatening anti-choice messages.

When I was a teenager, I used to say I was pro-choice but could never have an abortion myself. Being in the situation where I was pregnant and virtually alone, without a social network or the financial ability to support and care for a baby, and not able to imagine giving a child away, I am so thankful I could easily access an abortion. As much as I didn't "want" an abortion, I didn't feel it was fair to bring a child into my unstable life. And, in reality, since the beginning of time women have chosen to abort for a variety of reasons.

The only anti-choice influence came a couple months later, when I saw a billboard that read, "We regret our abortions," with a photo of a large group of women. That billboard really upset me. I wasn't upset because I regretted my abortion, but my emotions were still very conflicted. It was not an easy decision or one I enjoyed having to make. To me that billboard was mocking the difficult time I had with my choice. It seemed to be over-simplifying the issue, and that made me mad.

MIKA

I had my abortion when I was eighteen, four months ago. I was living with my boyfriend and working as a waitress.

My mom took me to the abortion, and my boyfriend did not want to go. My mom was really supportive. I needed that, and I wished my boyfriend had been there, especially when I chose to look at the ultrasound.

It was not hard for me to find the clinic—a friend and then my counselor told me everything I needed to know. I then waited a month for it. Waiting was hard because I was sick and working. I was very depressed.

There was a protester at the door of the clinic, an old man. I saw him and I felt so MAD at him that I just cried on the street.

I have heard my friends and family members talk about their abortions. It has helped me A LOT (IT WAS THE THING THAT HELPED ME THE MOST), because it helped me feel normal, and not ashamed as I did in the beginning.

I am pro-choice because I believe a woman should have the right to choose where, when, and how she will reproduce.

KALEIGH

I was twenty-six when I decided to have an abortion. The support I received during my abortion was pivotal to my health and well-being, though it did not come from traditional avenues. I told a few close friends and other women in my community whom I knew had had abortions. It was these women who provided the utmost support at this time. Hearing their stories, getting advice from them, and knowing that they would be there no matter what I needed was what saw me through the eight-and-a-half weeks of my pregnancy. It was reassurance that as alone as I felt, they had once felt that alone too.

Now, I talk about my abortion ALL THE TIME. When I was going through it, I hid it from most people both because I felt ashamed and because I was so tired and drained from the experience of being pregnant that I didn't want to deal with people. I just felt so isolated and I was sure no one would get it. Now that it is over and it means so much to me, I talk about it a lot. I have even lectured about it publicly. This is because I want other women to know that they are not alone, and because I believe that in having open conversations we actively annihilate shame.

Perhaps part of why I feel so strongly about speaking as a way of eliminating shame is because I am a person with a visible disability. For my entire life I have seen people look at me and wonder why I am different, but have been too afraid to ask. I always took their silence as an indicator that I should be ashamed of my difference, which I found insulting and untrue. Now, I take the silence around abortion in the same way—as indicative that I should be ashamed. Talking about it, therefore, works against this imposed societal value system.

LORI

He got all quiet and put his head down and sighed. Then he said, "Well, we can go back to Saskatchewan and get married. We can live on my Dad's farm. Or you can get an abortion." I looked at him for about three seconds and said I would have an abortion. The thing is—I had NO problem making that decision. It wasn't even a decision for me. I knew that was the thing to do. I felt it. I knew it was okay with the little thing growing in me (who wanted a fifteen-year-old mother who couldn't even break up with a guy she hated being with?). I knew it was okay with God. I prayed about it, I talked to God about it, and I knew inside of me that he/she was okay with it. This was not what I was supposed to be doing with my life right now. I was a kid myself.

It was 1972, and abortion was still not legal in most provinces. Fortunately in British Columbia it was, although it was not an easy process. I had to have my parents' consent since I was underage. THAT was the most traumatic part for me. Telling them was a nightmare. My mother went through the roof, and was very distraught and angry with me. My father cried and said nothing. My mother was determined to make me suffer for what I had done and felt abortion was an easy way out for me. She wanted to send me away somewhere to have the baby. It was terribly exhausting and upsetting. I had made up my mind and had intended to tell them what I was going to do—they took over and were telling ME what to do because now I had ruined their lives. It suddenly became about everyone else. NO ONE asked me how I felt, or what I wanted.

I still feel I made the best decision and I have no regrets about the abortion itself. I am happy that at this time in history, girls can have abortions without parental consent. My experience would have been entirely different had that been the case in '72. I knew what was right for me—women know what is right for them.

The support I would have appreciated: one kind word from anyone. When I counsel women at the clinic now, I use words like brave, wise, smart, and courageous. I do what I can to communicate to these women that making a choice like this is another step towards empowerment—that they are choosing for themselves.

ABOUT THE EDITOR

Martha Solomon is a British Columbia based educator, activist and writer. She has an MA in Women's Studies and History from the University of Toronto and has taught Philosophy and Women's Studies at the postsecondary level in both Canada and the US.

Passionate about social justice and equity, Martha is drawn to the intersection between art and activism. She is the co-founder of the award-winning arts4choice project, which has been exhibited in Toronto, Ottawa, Calgary, and Portland as well as published in the *Globe and Mail*. Martha has also directed a short documentary film about pro-choice activists.

ABOUT THE PHOTOGRAPHER

Kathryn Palmateer is a pro-choice photographer, filmmaker and activist. She has a degree in International Development from Dalhousie University and a Master's degree in Political Science from York University.

Kathryn runs a successful wedding photography and workshop business in Toronto. Her extensive experience in both lifestyle and portraiture emphasize a documentary style. She has travelled across Canada and the United States photographing women for the arts4choice project, as well as compiling a wide range of work on such diverse subjects as US War Resisters, Canadian Midwives and Breastfeeding Mothers.

Kathryn co-directed her first feature length comedy, *A Brand New You*, with her husband, which recently won a Gold Remi Award at WorldFest Houston 2014. She lives in Toronto with her three favourites, Shawn, Bea and Tilly.

ACKNOWLEDGEMENTS

Working at nights, during children's naps, from different countries and time zones, this project has been a labour of love. We would like to thank all of the participants who have contributed their stories to this book and to the arts4choice project—your generosity and courage in sharing your experiences is what this book is all about.

We'd also like to thank a few people and organizations that shared their ideas, time, talents, passion and, occasionally, funds, with us along the way, especially: Elizabeth Snell, Laura Parsons, Victoria Mata, Jessica Danforth, Michelle Robidoux and Carolyn Egan of OCAC, Joyce Arthur of ARCC, Karolina Walczak our amazing volunteer, Ayesha Adhami of the Immigrant Women's Health Center, the Ontario Arts Council, the National Abortion Federation, and all the abortion providers who provide women with compassionate care, CAW, CUPE3902 and 3903.

We'd also like to thank Judy Rebick and Jillian Bardsley for their insightful forewords to the book and especially Sarah Wayne, publisher at Three O'Clock Press, for patiently dealing with all our ideas and requests.

An extra special thanks to Wilson, from Martha. From that day in 2004 when I told you I just had to get on the OCAC bus to Washington and you said, "let's go!" to hashing out big ideas and reading drafts, your support and love has meant the world to me.

And from Kathryn, to my dear parents, your support means everything, whether it is travelling across the continent with the exhibit and screaming Bea or just your love and encouragement, and to Shawn, my partner in life, love, art and politics, thank you for everything.

RESOURCES

If you require abortion care or counseling, we urge you to talk to your doctor and/or call the Options Hotline by Canadians for Choice at 1-800-647-2725 or the National Abortion Federation hotline at 1-800-772-9100.

If you would like more information about getting involved in pro-choice activism, the National Abortion Federation (NAF) Canada and the Abortion Rights Coalition of Canada (ARCC) are great places to start.